MW01121927

CHILDREN OF GOD

Poems, dreams, and nightmares from
The Family of God Cult

By Craig DiLouie
and Jonathan Moon

The road to Hell
is paved ...

©2016 Craig DiLouie and Jonathan Moon. All rights reserved.

This is a work of fiction. All characters, events, and places portrayed in this novel are either fictitious or used fictitiously.

Scripture quotations are taken from the Holy Bible, New Living Translation, copyright ©1996, 2004, 2007 by Tyndale House Foundation. Used by permission of Tyndale House Publishers, Inc., Carol Stream, Illinois 60188.
All rights reserved.

No part of this book may be reproduced, stored in a retrieval system, or transmitted by any means without the written permission of the authors.

Cover design and interior formatting by Eloise J. Knapp
www.ekcoverdesign.com

Published by ZING Communications, Inc.
and Jonathan Moon.

www.CraigDiLouie.com

www.MrMoonBlogs.blogspot.com

THE CHILDREN OF GOD

CULT.

Defined as group veneration of a specific person, object, or belief system.

From the Latin, *cultus*, meaning "worship."

It's a powerful word. But still tough to define.

Cults form around many figures and beliefs, from one centered on a man who claimed to be a 500-year-old vampire to others dedicated to UFOs, but many are religious groups.

So what's the difference between a religious cult and a church?

A religion describes a religious belief and system of worship. These beliefs may be mainstream, or they may be something new. Sociologists dub the latter a new religious movement, not a cult.

What makes a group a *cult* in the popular sense is how strange and sinister most people find its beliefs, and how destructively it behaves towards its members and community.

Because, in the end, all cults are harmful.

There are as many as 5,000 cults operating in the United States.

*

Studies reveal that all cults have several common characteristics: Fanatical veneration of a person or belief system. Program to socialize new members and create emotional dependency on the group. Indoctrination toward a new worldview. Ultimately doing harm to its members and possibly the community. Isolation, exploitation, mind control, abuse.

And, for some, destruction.

*

The group may require recruits to cut themselves off from friends and family, prove instant and unquestioning obedience to strict rules, and work hard with little sleep. All of which is designed to manipulate the individual into unquestioning loyalty and dependency. That, and:

Destroy their sense of self and replace it with the leader's vision and will. Get them to give up everything for the group and become completely dependent on it. And get them to cede all control to the group mind, which is to say, its leader's.

If the member disobeys or otherwise gains disapproval of the group, its greatest punishment is banishment from its security, community, and promises.

While cults are protected by the First Amendment of the Constitution, the fact that they're harmful is no secret in America. It's popular knowledge that various cults have performed abuse, murder, mass suicide.

Heaven's Gate. The People's Temple. The Family. Twelve Tribes. Why would anyone join one?

The easy answer is these people are defective in some way.

They're crazy.

Studies point to a different view.

*

Cult recruiters seek out the displaced.

A woman going through divorce. A man who's lost his job. A woman seeking greater meaning in her faith. A man who's tired of being alone.

These people come from all walks of life. All classes, many professions, all levels of education.

They may feel alienated from society.

They may feel lonely.

They may be shy and inhibited.

They're often angry at a world that doesn't make sense.

The group offers answers. A simple worldview that makes everything click. A sense of being special. A sense of purpose, excitement, friendship and family, a mission. Meaning.

Once initiation is complete, they're transformed.

In the end, they become people willing to suffer for the greater good, people who see themselves as superior to society while being afraid of it. Fear that they channel back into love for the group and its leader.

And here's a funny thing.

They never believed they were joining a "cult."

*

Sometimes, they're banished. That, or they drop out.

After leaving, many become depressed. They feel guilty. They're afraid. They stop caring.

They may even miss their old life in the group's warm, loving chains.

They may leave the cult, but for many, the cult never leaves them.

*

This psychological background is essential to understanding the Christian doomsday cult Family of God and those who survived the nightmarish mass suicide and massacre on August 17, 2008.

In the aftermath of the 9/11 terrorist attacks, David Prince began preaching the apocalypse was coming fast. He gathered a group of disciples and formed a church in Los Angeles.

The Temple of the Family of God.

His reading of the Book of Revelation had led him to believe God would end the world with fire but would spare 144,000. Only they would achieve immortality and enjoy the fruits of the new covenant Jesus Christ had made with humanity. Like Noah, Prince had been chosen to lead these people to salvation from the wrath and build a new world blessed by Christ's return.

The Kingdom of Heaven, realized on the earth.

You were either in, or you were out. God had given humanity free will to choose to become one of the elect who would survive and live in the returned kingdom.

Many heard the call, only a few came. Those who did were the chosen.

At the time, the church offered strong fellowship and love to its initiates, though that love was conditional on shared belief and reverence for Prince himself. Many opted to live together. Even then, darkness had seeped into the edges of the community. They loved but also judged each other based on how observant they were of their shared beliefs.

At its peak, the Family of God boasted more than 2,000 members. Not nearly enough. Prince began to believe other Noahs were gathering the rest of the 144,000 from around the world.

In any case, America had been given its chance to board the ark. The fire was coming.

*

On, June 13, 2004, Prince led his followers to Tehachapi Mountain, the high point of the Tehachapi Mountains in eastern California.

There, they awaited the end of the world.

And today was the day.

God had destroyed the world once with a flood, now with fire. A purification that would lead to a renewal of the earth.

Only a few would survive. Only a few had been chosen. It would be a terrible day for the world, but for these elect few, it would be a day of victory and deliverance.

On this mountain, they'd welcome Christ's return and receive his blessing.

But it didn't happen. They all went home wondering why.

Once they'd returned to Los Angeles, some of Prince's followers left the church. Many had become so dedicated, however, that they only found their beliefs strengthened. By now, they acted on feelings, not thought.

Months later, their leader brought nearly 450 of them back to land purchased near the mountain. The end was still imminent, so they had to be ready at all times.

There, the hardships began. The isolation.

The brutality.

And the process that ultimately led to the violent death of 382 people.

Three years, they waited.

Subsistence farming in the desert. Endless hard work followed by hours of prayer and lectures by Prince on what awaited at the end of their long, hard road.

They lived at the edge of starvation but saw themselves as kings.

God's chosen.

In or out, and nobody gets in without being tested.

Some trickled away, but most stayed.

They forgot their hunger in hosannas.

By accepting the promise of Heaven, the members had made their last act of free will. The stakes were too high to allow dissension. Prince created a hierarchy of favorites. The Fishers, his inner council. The Watchers, who were allowed to carry weapons and roamed the barbed wire fences at night. The Little Angels, children walking among the squalor in their white robes.

Near Tehachapi Mountain, the Family of God became a cult.

Mind control. Hard labor. Severe discipline. Harsh punishments. Isolation. Paranoia. Torture. Disfigurement.

All for the greater good.

All to become perfect enough for Jesus to come.

The mountain is named for a Native American word that means "the hard climb."

Prince called it, and the community he'd built, Masada. He renamed it after the legendary fortress in Israel, a place of safety and refuge.

There, for another seven months, he broke his followers one by one, and once they were broken, he had a new vision.

They were to leave the earth before the fire came.

They needed to die for the apocalypse to arrive.

Their kingdom awaited in Heaven.

*

Cyanide, arsenic, barbiturates mixed with fruit punch and vodka.

Plastic bags pulled over their heads to ensure death through asphyxiation.

Some drank willingly, but others didn't want to die.

Prince pitied them. If he'd loved them any less, he might have let them go. But after everything they'd been through together, he couldn't leave them behind. They were his subjects in the Kingdom of Heaven, and they were coming with him.

He ordered them killed by the Watchers.

Automatic rifles to gun them down at the barbed wire.

Axes to cut off their heads.

Fire to set Prince alight.

The slaughter lasted all night.

Nine had already died during the preceding months. That last night, 373 more. Men, women, children. Their lives, loves, hopes, hates, dreams, all gone forever.

Only thirty-one survived.

*

The cable news carried lurid around-the-clock coverage of the aftermath. Police tape, shell casings, bodies linked arm in arm, blood-soaked dirt. The rescue and arrests. Breathless anchors and guests condemned cults and issued stern warnings. Everywhere, people were shocked. They talked about it for days.

They saw the Family of God as a bunch of lunatics.

They wondered how anybody could be so gullible, stupid, and self-destructive.

Then they forgot all about it.

＊

Of the thirty-one survivors, two were sentenced to life in prison for murder. The rest were handed back to their families, all of them scarred physically and mentally. Most still reside in psychiatric hospitals.

Nobody said a word about what had happened for years.

Many couldn't speak at all after what they'd suffered at Masada.

Many still believed the end was coming.

Eight finally did their part and committed suicide.

In 2009, Dr. Patricia Salazar, a psychiatrist in Pittsburgh who'd treated former cult members, took an interest in the Family of God survivors, who had all been diagnosed with severe post-traumatic stress disorder.

PTSD occurs when an individual is exposed to a stressful event or period that overwhelms his or her ability to cope with it. It inhibits the ability to regulate memory and subsequent emotional response.

Sufferers re-experience their trauma, become aggressive and hyper vigilant, and have difficulties with memory and learning.

Some also disassociate—suffer an uncoupling of the mind from their emotional state and, in some cases, their bodies.

Dr. Salazar had an idea on how to break through to the Family of God survivors.

＊

Poetry therapy became formalized in the 1980s as a way to treat PTSD. Dr. Salazar had been using poetry therapy to treat PTSD in Iraq War veterans, and she'd achieved good results.

The National Association for Poetry Therapy promotes its use for "healing and personal growth." Poetry therapy has several key goals, including developing a deeper understanding of self, enabling self-expression, venting overwhelming emotions and memories, and facilitating change and coping.

One theory about treatment of PTSD is to restore the patient's sense of control, allowing them to experience life with feelings of safety and hope.

Recovery takes three steps. First, recognize the problem and stop the bleeding. Second, recall the details of the traumatic memory. Third, reconnect with themselves.

Connect with their present emotions. Gain control. Rebuild.

The therapist engaged the survivors. Of the twenty-three living survivors, fifteen responded. The survivors learned about poetry and completed exercises from *The Journal to the Self* (Adams, 1999). They wrote poems in regular sessions and, after each session, completed a questionnaire that asked questions about their emotional state and behavioral changes.

The goal was to express themselves, with no right or wrong way to do it.

The results were extraordinary.

*

The survivors laid bare their souls in free verse, villanelles, haiku, found poetry, sonnets, and rap lyrics. At first, the poems focused on how the survivors were feeling, with the intent being to find a strong positive concept.

Over time, the survivors were encouraged to explore their memories.

Eleven did.

In the end, the program achieved some success. Five of the

eleven were able to gain a greater sense of safety and control, regulate their internal states more effectively, and connect with and trust people who were not Family of God members. For them, the questionnaires suggested improvement in their self-esteem and ability to engage with life in the present. They were able to reintegrate with society and are now living functional, happier lives.

The rest showed positive outcomes for trauma recovery but could not shake the guilt that they'd survived. They'd left the Family of God, but the Family of God may never leave them. They're still waiting for the apocalypse. Some are still trying to die.

*

In 2016, Dr. Salazar contacted the editors of this collection and asked them to edit and prepare it for publication, with permission from the cult members. Their church names are used in this book instead of their real names.

In this collection of poems, the survivors of more than three years of brutality and the horrifying night of August 17, 2008 finally find their voice and have their say.

Why they joined the group. What they wanted, hoped, believed.

And in hearing their voices and listening to their stories, readers may come to understand not just what happened, but why.

Because the story of the Family of God isn't just about a single night of horror. It isn't just about people united in a search for utopia and subsequent plunge into madness. It's a story about love, longing, and faith. About people searching for meaning and acting on it. About people a lot like us.

Though the results were horribly tragic, they thought they

were finding God.

Right to the end, they thought they'd been chosen.

*

The Family of God was a Christian doomsday cult. These cults are particularly fascinating because of the juxtaposition between genuine Christian love, community, and yearning for meaning against the horror of murder and suicide as the group's aspirations reach a climax.

Beyond a basic biography, not much is known of David Prince. Middle class, college dropout, bounced between jobs and churches. Prince was as restless as his followers, always in transition, constantly searching for something.

Many cult leaders are essentially charismatic narcissists who form groups to serve themselves, but Prince may not fit that mold, at least not initially. By all accounts, he was a man with a genuine faith in God, and he sought a deeper meaning in that relationship. A man with an intense personal struggle. Throughout it all, he worked and suffered alongside his followers, sharing their pain.

After forming his commune near Tehachapi Mountain, however, Prince became a monster. The promise of salvation from God's wrath turned into a time of testing. The more they were tested, the more they earned salvation. If their eye caused them to sin, it was plucked out. Everybody sacrificed something. Nobody escaped whole. Most gave willingly. The more intense their suffering, the stricter their observance of God's laws, the more likely Jesus would return.

In Prince's mind, he was helping his people find God. He thought he was saving them. One thing we can know for certain about him, he was a true believer with an interpretation of Scripture that had a consistent and precise internal logic.

11

These beliefs led them all to a horrifying end.

But this isn't his story.

It's the story of those who followed him.

CONTRIBUTORS

ARIEL: A toddler when her mother first joined the Family of God, she basically grew up in the congregation. She was six in August 2008, one of the "Little Angels," the name given children not old enough to work.

JEDIDIAH: A seminary student living in Los Angeles, he met David Prince shortly after the September 11 attacks and joined the Family of God. During the years at Masada, the group's compound in eastern California, he became the most energetic of the "Fishers"—a group of twelve men and women who essentially ran the group under Prince's direction.

ELIZABETH: A young prostitute and heroin user who'd become a born-again Christian after a failed suicide attempt, Elizabeth joined the congregation in 2003.

RUTH: At 74 years of age when she joined the Family of God in 2002, Ruth, abandoned by her sons who'd sold her home for cash and put her into a senior living facility, was the group's oldest member.

TOBY: Mentally impaired, Toby had lived with his parents and worked odd jobs well into his 30s, when he began working for the Family of God. He joined the congregation in 2002.

MARY: Mary worked in a flower shop and played organ for her local church well into her 40s, when she joined the Family of God after a friend invited her to hear David Prince deliver a sermon. She played the organ during services and helped Prince with church administration, though she never became a Fisher.

DINAH: Another of the Little Angels, Dinah joined the Family of God after her mother—who'd bounced from man to man and town to town after fleeing an abusive marriage—fell in love with one of the group's members.

JOSHUA: The son of Russian immigrants who died tragically in an auto accident, this highly sensitive and intelligent young man turned away from his faith and searched for meaning until finding the Family of God in 2003.

GABRIEL: An LA gangbanger, Gabriel and several of his friends joined the Family of God in 2002. During the last year at Masada, Gabriel and several other members of the congregation were armed and appointed "Watchers," a group that enforced the rules of Prince and the Fishers and otherwise patrolled the barbed wire enclosure.

JARED: A street tough given the choice of jail or Iraq, Jared served with distinction, though he left the country wounded physically and psychologically. He joined the Family of God in mid-2004.

THE WORD: Selected texts from the Holy Bible's Book of Revelation that were given special emphasis in David Prince's writings. These passages are presented as he wrote them out in his notebooks.

ARIEL

Ah! A desert wind
How pleasing its chill as it
Brings the final screams

IN THE BEGINNING

September 2001 to June 2004

THE WORD

Look! He comes with the clouds of heaven.

And everyone will see him—

even those who pierced him.

And all the nations of the world

will mourn for him.

Yes! Amen!

—Revelation 1:7

JEDIDIAH

The planes struck the buildings,

Then everything changed.

It was bigger than all of us.

We didn't know what it meant,

The buildings coming down in dust.

It was big, so big, it hurt.

People held hands and cried,

Watched scrolling terror alerts.

It felt bigger than history itself.

David said he understood the signs,

Pointing down the road of apocalypse.

That was bigger than anything.

Many would be called but few would listen,

Even fewer would be chosen.

An idea even bigger than your skepticism.

The fire that would end the world

Started as a spark in my heart.

I became part of something far bigger than me.

ELIZABETH

"My Rock, Jesus"

God warms the sinner but against sin freezes,
Cold as dead was I in my life of Cain.
The fall was so long, I broke into pieces.

Spread legs, sucked cock, provided what pleases,
All to push cheer into my thirsty vein.
Hit rock bottom, but that rock was Jesus.

My man wanted other men's wealth that teases,
We killed, we took our wage and left the stain.
The fall was so long, I broke into pieces.

Trapped in a thirst that drinks but ne'er ceases,
I no longer filled but opened my vein.
Hit rock bottom, but that rock was Jesus.

I fell into dark where light ne'er reaches,

Departed a life ruled by pleasure and pain,

The fall was so long, I broke into pieces.

God saved me for wonder that ne'er ceases,

His Temple embraced me with love and chain,

Hit rock bottom, but that rock was Jesus.

The fall was so long, I broke into pieces.

RUTH

"These Old Eyes"

These old eyes
Have cry'd and cry'd
A mother's tears
Of pain and pride.

These old eyes
How they weep'd
Gazin' 'pon
My babies each.

These old eyes
Watch'd babes grow
Much to teach,
Much to know.

These old eyes
Strained old with life
Raised greedy boys
Who got greedy wives.

These old eyes

Watched their home

Get sold away

And me left alone.

These old eyes

Stared too long

At drab old walls

That looked so wrong.

These old eyes

Grew tired and blind

To the sight of kin

And the past behind.

These old eyes

Have cry'd and cry'd

A mother's tears

Of pain and pride.

TOBY

The Temple of the Family of God is pleased to present:
THE POWER OF CHRIST'S LOVE
An evening of worship, live music and fellowship

Make friends!
Rejoice in God!
Live better!

"Here I am! I stand at the door and knock.
If anyone hears my voice and opens the door, I will come in
And eat with that person, and they with me."
– Revelation 3:20

Services every Saturday until His return
Potluck dinner at 5:30, services start at 7:00 PM

Admission free

ARIEL

Cry, shout, scream, run—go!
The children play while upstairs
Mommy sings to God

MARY

"Songs of Solomon"

I played the organ every night,
So good it made the sinners mew.
Love songs to God to ease their plight,
Sometimes I played them just for you.

O Dav'd, my soul felt close to God
Whene'er we so humbly prayed.
Dear Sol, my flesh felt pretty awed,
When you cast eyes at this old maid.

Sometimes, I dreamt my bleeding fists
Like Thomas touched your mortal form.
Though God my soul with beauty kissed
Saw fit my body to deform.

My soul found thrill, my flesh no vice,
Forever am I wed to Christ.

RUTH

"Come to Grandma Now"

Look at all the lost children,
So broken an' dismay'd,
Gather'd by our shepherd great
To rejoice in love this day.

Come to Grandma now,
Let me love you like my own.

We've all braved the storms,
So terrible an' lonely,
To find our shepherd kind
An' form this bless'd family.

Come to Grandma now,
Let our love build our home.

Look at the lost children,
Reborn now in the light,

Guided by our shepherd brave
An' deliver'd through the night.

Come to Grandma now,
And we'll never be alone.

We've all suffer'd badness,
An' we made it through,
In the arms of our shepherd modest,
Our love, it grew an' grew.

Come to Grandma now,
Let God's work be done.

Look at the Lord's children,
All gather'd now around me,
At the grace of our shepherd holy
We'll rise up for the Lord to see.

Come to Grandma now,
Let me love you like my own.

DINAH

"Echoes of a Broken Childhood"

I remember trying to watch TV
While daddy yelled at Mommy.
He'd shout,
She'd whimper.
The sounds of their voices
Echo in my mind
A cartoon scream with a laugh track.

I remember trying to color
While Daddy beat up Mommy.
As if his words
Didn't hurt enough.
The sounds of fist pounding meat
Echo in my mind
As I shake too hard to color in the lines.

I remember trying to braid Dolly's hair

While Mommy explained why Daddy hurt.

It's just how

Your daddy loves, she said.

The sounds of her excuses

Echo in my mind

While I pull out Dolly's hair.

I remember trying to make new friends

While Mommy outran Daddy.

He was really mad

So we moved a lot.

The sounds of highways

Echo in my mind

While I look for those friends.

I remember trying to understand

Why Mommy suffered Daddy.

Mommy still cried

The day Daddy died.

The sounds of her wailing

Echo in my mind

As the more I lost, the more I learned.

I remember trying to be a child

While nothing stayed the same.

The bruises she gave me faded

When she'd find love again.

The sounds of my youth

Echo still in my mind

Until I'd given up my childhood.

ELIZABETH

"Perfection's Price"

Jesus, you accept me every day,
But a better woman I want to be.
Feel all the pain, then take it away.

They made you suffer with their cruel play,
Naked, broken, scorned, and bloody.
Perfection's a price the body must pay.

You showed me the road, you showed me the way,
Until back home, crawling on scraped hands and
knees.
Feel all the pain, then take it away.

You suffered, as I'd, our scars on display,
Those scars made us close, allowed me to see
Perfection's a price the body must pay.
Make me earn your love, and I will obey,

Beauty outside, ugly inside, I'm awful, truly.
Feel all the pain, then take it away.

So Lord, though you love me without dismay,
I crave crucifixion on the same tree.
Perfection's a price the body must pay.
Feel all the pain, then take it away.

JOSHUA

They proudly call her Mother Russia,

And she holds a nation of millions

To her freezing teats.

They say there is such great beauty

In her mountains and valleys

None would want to stray.

So, how terrible was the Krakow ghetto

To chase my parents away

From their loving Motherland

Into the arms of a stranger?

They proudly call it the Land of Opportunity,

And it holds up a nation of millions

To dream their million dreams.

They say here everyone is welcome

To share in the prosperity

That all have a right to.

So, how terrible was the rush hour traffic

To crush my parents away

In broken glass and tangled steel

And ruin their dream forever?

They proudly call it an act of charity

And they deliver broken children aplenty

Into homes so welcoming.

They say that wounds can heal

With time and love,

The comfort of a safe home,

So, how terrible was my foster care

To crush my innocence

With rape and daily bruises

From my heinous caregivers?

They proudly call it a life of sobriety

And the good people all live

With a natural happy high.

They say the power is inside

Our individual selves

Given by a higher power.

So, how terrible was my weak soul

To need the numbing blur

Of heroin and crack cocaine,

My only steadfast lovers?

They proudly call it the gift of life

And grateful should we all be

For our time upon the earth.

They say it is what you make of it

And each last one of us

Has choices and chances.

So, how terrible is the world

With its lifelong lies and brutal truths

Of hope and dreams

And the happiness of anything?

MARY

"God's Gifts"

I may be fat and unlovely to see,
But I am on good speaking terms with God.
Though I may long to lose this gross body,
My organ playing made angels applaud.

In his wisdom, God made all men special,
I poured love songs on the altar for Christ.
Harmonies for worship, melodies for revel,
A song can please more than blood sacrifice.

God bestows gifts, yes, but if we take pride,
As the Lord gives, he can and will take away.
Better to lose a hand than cast aside,
Better return the gift than led astray.

Jesus took our prayers, he took our love,
But didn't come; we just weren't pure enough.

DINAH

"Mommy Loved a Man Who Loved Jesus"

I slept in hotel beds
When Mommy was alone.
I slept in the stains of
Others' sweat and sorrow.

The tired traveler is not the scared girl,
But they toss and turn just the same way.

I slept on strangers' couches
When Mommy had her boyfriends.
I'd play with neighbor kids
While Mommy moaned in bed.

The lonely woman is not the abusive mom,
But they inflict pain just the same way.

I began sleeping in just one bed

When Mommy loved a man who loved Jesus.

I slept warm and deep,

Comfortably safe while Mommy snored.

We found a family, not at all like our family,

And we would never, ever stray again.

GABRIEL

"The Ark"

Praise Jesus
What?
Praise Jesus
What?
Praise the **Lord** Jesus
WHAT?

I'll say it again, see, I got no shame

I was tired, tired of the same old game

Trick and treat, treat and trick

Days for my money, nights for my dick

Mine was life at the edge where all light had fled

One more day on the street and I'd have ended up dead

It was no way to live, like my ma always said

That street was a beast that screamed to be fed

The street ain't the type that you'd want to abuse

It made me a deal that I couldn't refuse

To be a fighter, a marshal, a runner of crews

A sword, a shield, a counter of coups

But I was searching hard for something pure

My soul was roaming, I needed a cure

Didn't know it was God until God found me

God needed my help 'cause he's got this enemy

You know I never strayed from a tussle

God was hurting and He needed some muscle

Satan was loose and deserves all the blame

God was getting set to get rid of this game

The Lord ain't the type that you'd want to abuse

He made me a deal that I couldn't refuse

45

To be a watcher, a shepherd, a spreader of news

A savior, a king, a solver of clues

The Reverend, he said, why be king for a day

Join me now, son, and I'll show you the way

To be king for a life, a life that won't end

Join the Elect and it's you I will send

To be a watcher, a shepherd, a spreader of news

A fighter, a marshal, a runner of crews

A savior, a king, a solver of clues

A sword, a shield, a counter of coups

I'll say it clear, so I don't confuse

I was Noah bringing sheep to the Ark in their twos

I was fighting God's fight, so what's your excuse

When God burns you, don't be moaning the blues

Praise Jesus
What?
Praise Jesus
What?
Praise the **Lord** Jesus
WHAT?

You fucking heard me, son.

TOBY

"Just As I Am" pp. 77-78
"Everybody's Friend" pp. 41-43
"A Shelter in Time of Storm" pp. 91-93
"Are You Washed in the Blood?" pp. 105-106
"Are You Ready?" pp. 99-100

CHRISTIAN HYMNS
Published by God's Word Printing Company, Inc.
P.O. Box 2000
Rosebud, Nebraska 68501-2000

Copyright © 1986, 1991, 1999.
All rights reserved.

No part of this book may be
        reproduced
or transmitted
        in any form
or by any electronic
        or mechanical means
including information storage
        and retrieval systems
without written permission
        from the publisher.

Printed in the
        United
                States of
                        America

JARED

"For God and Country"

I was a soldier in an army of boys.

Vatos Locos, Ese,

My clique,

My childhood,

My crimes.

Blue bandanas and 9 mm toys.

I was a soldier in an army of men.

Ratta-tat-tat,

My gun,

My garrison,

My glory.

I fought for freedom in the sand.

I was a soldier bold and brave.

Incoming!

My people,

My peace of mind,

My pain.

My friends died, I was saved.

I was a soldier wounded and discarded.

Why did they die while I lived?

My home,

My hospital,

My hope.

Walk with a limp, so broken-hearted.

I was a soldier broken twice.

Dark alleys were my home.

My bedroom,

My bathroom,

My birthright.

Cold and alone, until I found Christ.

I was a soldier for God and country.

Ratta-tat-tat,

My gun,

My glory,

My God.

But only the Lord stands by me.

DINAH

Mommy had a testimony,

And, Lord,

She loved to share it.

Her eyes got teary,

Her voice got choked,

As she retold our story,

Every beating,

Every scream,

Until I was crying too.

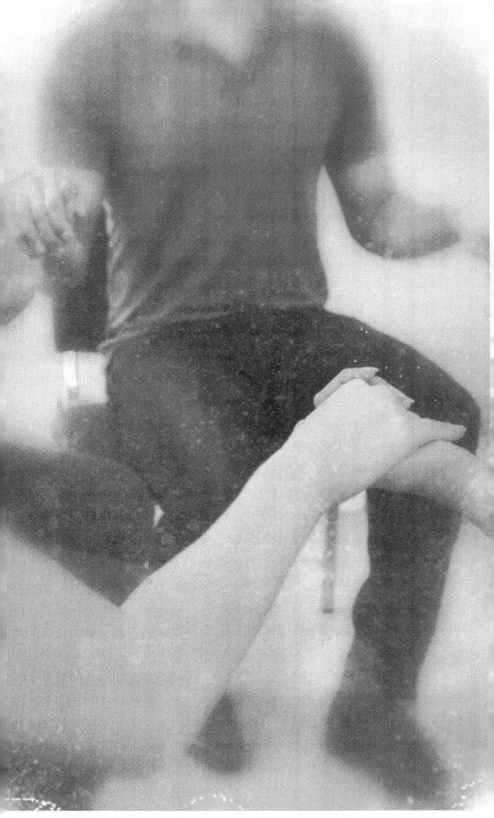

JOSHUA

"The Father Calls" (A Chant)

So many faces turning to the light

With looks of desperation

Glowing in their eyes.

Staggering weak as newborn fawns

Amazed by each sunset,

Awed by every dawn.

The Father calls his children home,

The faithful and the true.

The Father calls his children home,

He calls to me and you.

So many children survived the long night

With looks of salvation

Tearing in their eyes.

Saved are we and pressing on

Sharing the great word,

Saving the foregone.

The Father calls his children home,

The faithful and the true.

The Father calls his children home,

He calls to me and you.

So many people smiling bright

With looks of devotion

Showing in their eyes.

Closed doors we knock upon

Preaching word of Jesus,

And gospels of John.

The Father calls his children home,

The faithful and the true.

The Father calls his children home,

He calls to me and you.

So many hypocrites frightful of the light

With looks of revulsion

Simmering in their eyes.

Refused, refuted, we carry on

In our hearts the Lord,

On our lips this song:

The Father calls his children home,

The faithful and the true.

The Father calls his children home,

He calls to me and you.

MARY

"Helping Hurts"

Responsibility is hard,
David knew that better than all.
But on those nights he'd had enough,
I was the one who broke his fall.

I would massage his weary feet,
Some nights I'd lick them up and down.
And when I couldn't take the heat,
He'd scold my sin with his dark frown.

Being the one who helps can hurt,
Hurt so bad that you can't help more.
Apocalypse always came first,
For this great man whom I adored.

O David, I helped as best I could,
I wished you'd let me as I would.

JARED

"Something to Believe In"

Mom and Dad gave me

A white boy's name,

Though they are

Black and brown.

They moved me to

Where the schools

Were better,

On the whiter side of town.

Uncle Sam gave me

A rifle in my hand,

A welcome option to

The courts plan.

He moved me to

Where dangers

Lurked

Across a foreign land.

The Reverend Price gave me

The greatest gift ever given.

My kind shepherd

Saved my soul,

And the Temple

Took me in.

Finally, I had

Something to believe in.

flesh.

24 Now unto him that h
keep you from falling, and
sent you faultless before the
of his glory with exceeding

25 To the only wise Go
viour, be glory and maj
nion and power, both
Amen.

e Spirit.

them-

un-

re

me,

REVELATIO

OF

ST. JOHN THE DIVINE.

TER I.
elation to the seven churches
by the seven golden candle-
ng of Christ. 14 His glorious

lation of Jesus Christ,
God gave unto him, to
his servants things which
come to pass; and he
d it by his angel

of the kings
that loved
our sins
6 And
priests
him
and
7

ARIEL

Folding chairs close, *clack*!

Grownups chatter, crowd the door

Lights out, now God sleeps

JEDIDIAH

I was training to be a firefighter
In a burning house.
That's why I gave up seminary.

I was training to be a cop
During a rape and robbery.
That's why I left it all behind.

I wanted to become a warrior
During history's greatest war.
I heard a greater calling.

David instead made me a fisher of men,
And a shepherd to the human race.
My ministry was to save the world.

When our ranks swelled to two thousand,
David said the end was near.
We didn't leave, we'd arrived.
And nothing was going to stop us from saving the world.

AND THEY
SANG
A NEW
SONG
BEFORE THE THRONE AND BEFORE THE FOUR
LIVING CREATURES AND THE
ELDERS
NO ONE
COULD
LEARN THE
SONG
EXCEPT THE
144,000
WHO HAD
BEEN
REDEEMED
FROM THE
EARTH

—Revelation 14:3

COME, JESUS

June 2004 to January 2005

ARIEL

Caterpillar cars

Crawling toward the mountain

Gettin' set to fly

TOBY

Blue sky

Eagle

Hills like a big wrinkly blanket

Green scrub

Baked dirt

Orange dirt

Yellow dirt

Big rocks

Hot road

Crushed snake

Guard rail

Median

Mojave

Mountain we called

Masada

Masada

MASADA

THE WORD

Then the seventh angel

Blew his trumpet,

And there were loud voices

Shouting in heaven:

> "The world has now become the
> Kingdom of our Lord
> And of his Christ,
>> and he will reign forever and ever."

—Revelation 11:15

RUTH

"Let Our Voices Call Forth Paradise"

We the chosen gathered,
Waitin' on our Lord.
We sang our songs of glory,
Of sacrifice, reward.

How strong our voices sound'd,
Risin' to the sky.
Echoin' out this Earthy realm,
To reach great God on high.

We clap'd our hands an' shout'd,
So overcome with joy.
Tears from e'ery man an' woman,
Smiles on e'ery girl an' boy.

We danced an' pray'd an' sang,

Callin' forth our Lord.

Perhaps he could not hear us,

Or did not feel adored.

Our flock began to scatter,

The faithless takin' leave.

The faithful we remained,

Voices ringin' through dark eve.

The sun rose up again,

We knew we'd been deceived.

Half the camp was empty,

How little they'd believed.

Our Lord had seen us there,

The faithless in our ranks.

Their voices taintin' songs

Sung up to call his grace.

His anger is the fury,

But great mercy he performs.

Upon his beloved faithful,

Bravin' through the storm.

We'll pray again, an' sing again',

Callin' forth our Lord.

We'll sing our sounds of glory,

Of sacrifice, reward.

MARY

"Wedding Day"

The sinners walk'd up to the mount,
In new white robes they came to pray.
Two thousand 'fore I lost all count,
To witness there my wedding day.

Come, Jesus Christ, we call on you
To take your bride and claim your crown.
Your lady stands so proud and tall,
But pride, it can and will fall down.

Your blood washed all my sins away,
But failed to scrub my soul of pride.
You want perfection in e'ery way,
A broken, humble, bleeding bride.

First time I stood without a falter,
I was left jilted at the altar.

JOSHUA

"The Disappointment of the Long Night"

I was a believer in the desert.

There I sang and bled and prayed

To a god who wasn't listening,

To a god I found familiar.

And even with hundreds of others

Singing and bleeding and praying

The skies refused to open,

The night dragged on and on,

The sun it rose again,

Breaking many hearts.

My sunburn felt cooled

By the long night's breeze,

But my soul

Was sensing false relief.

The voices were desperate,

The prayers increasingly frantic,

How frightened they were

Of disappointment.

I was a believer as the faithless fled

I remained to sing and bleed and pray

To a god who wasn't listening,

To a god I found familiar.

Perhaps that's really why

Singing and bleeding and praying

My faith remained unshaken.

The slave too accustomed to

The weight of the shackle

To ever be free.

The spouse accepting the blame

For their own beating.

The junkie only seeing the world

Reflected in a burning spoon.

My voice has always been desperate,

My prayers have always been frantic.

How accustomed I have grown

To disappointment.

JEDIDIAH

"The Day the World Didn't End"

Some say we suffered great embarrassment

The day the world didn't end,

But I wonder …

Did they see the oceans of people

Praying under the sun?

Did they feel the ground shake and

Rumble with song?

Did they feel the air electric?

Fools will tell you nothing happened

The day the world didn't end,

But I wonder …

What do they know of faith and

The true cost of devotion?

What do followers of dollar signs

Know of love and emotion?

Do they feel humility as pain?

The televisions told of how we failed

The day the world didn't end,

But I wonder …

What would they have felt inside

Praying with the multitude?

Would such community destroy

The shackles of solitude?

Or is it all about the headlines?

Some said our fates were sealed

The day the world didn't end,

But I wonder …

Would the cleave away a limb

If it festered and rotted?

Could they cast out the faithless

As if it had been planned and plotted?

Would they follow a prophet to a mountain?

Some dared declare our prophet false

The day the world didn't end,

But I know …

They never saw the light in his soul

As it shimmered in his eyes.

They never heard his words

Infused with the power of the Lord.

They know not true holy.

ELIZABETH

"Line in the Sand"

Invited to feast, given empty plates,

The hungry Christians, they raged at their plight.

The crowd, it seethed like a river in spate.

Desert to river, love into hate,

The Christians gave up as day turned to night.

The line in the sand, it ran until late.

Why bring food when there is no wait?

Why bring water with the end in sight?

The crowd, it seethed like a river in spate.

They were promised by God, cheated by fate,

Bonfires burned as they started their flight.

The line in the sand, it ran until late.

David came down to confront the irate,

Headlights glared as some started to fight.

The crowd, it seethed like a river in spate.

They expected David to correct the date,

Instead drew a line and then turned aside.

The line in the sand, it ran until late.

The crowd, it seethed like a river in spate.

GABRIEL

"The Chaff and the Wheat"

The Reverend wept as he watched them fly
Each one a lost sheep believing he'd lied
The pain on his face, it was something to see
A holy man stuck in hellish misery

He had a staff, he drew a line in the sand
That was the Reverend making his stand
Those who stayed would be eating the bread
Those who crossed would be joining the dead

Didn't bother me none to lose our weaker half
Moses wasn't nice to his own with his staff
Now we'd see who'd have the last laugh
This is how God cuts the wheat from the chaff

At the top of a hill, we gathered around

The Reverend said, this here is holy ground

We're gonna come back to give Christ what he's needing

We're gonna turn this desert to a beautiful Eden

At the foot of Masada, it'll be our place

To wait until the Lord comes to give us his grace

Only the pure can enter the kingdom of Christ

Strong enough and willing to sacrifice

When the king comes, I'll be making a meet

When the kingdom comes, I'll be taking my seat

Those who'd left would be feeling the heat

This is how God cuts the chaff from the wheat

JEDIDIAH

Imagine if I said to you
I'm coming to your house
But didn't show up
You'd be mad

But then you'd remember
That I said to wait for me
I said to be ready
I said I was coming now

So if you loved me
Really loved me
You'd wait
You'd stay ready
And it would always be now

MASADA

February 2005 to August 2008

ELIZABETH

"A Time for Testing"

Our hopes all went up bye and bye,
Like smoke that follows quenched flame,
And Jesus never told us why.

On clouds we hoped to see him fly,
To scorch the earth and Satan tame.
Our hopes, they went up to the sky.

Too good for truth—but not a lie,
The path to reign required more pain,
And Jesus never told us why.

No point in grief, no cause to cry,
We had to earn what we would claim.
Our hopes, they went up to the sky.

While true, God left us high and dry,

Only through tears we might attain,
And Jesus never told us why.

By grace we were allowed retry,
With testing, we might break the chains.
Our hopes, they went up to the sky.
And Jesus never told us why.

JEDIDIAH

If you fail to love,
Do you stop trying?

If you fail to be good,
Do you give up?

We were trying to enter Heaven.
You don't just walk away from that.

So we went back to the mountain
To build a community.

We named it Masada, like the mountain we loved.
In the desert, we waited.

If at first you don't succeed,
You try again.

It wasn't us waiting,
It was God.

TOBY

Speed Limit 70
Radar Enforced

Truck Lane
Slow Vehicles Only

Slower Traffic
Keep Right

Avoid Overheating
Turn Off A/C Next 16 Miles

Rest Area
Two Miles

Warning
Narrow Road

Warning
Danger

RUTH

"Sunrise upon the Mountain"

My heart was so heavy,
Weigh'd down with
Troubl'd thoughts
When we arriv'd
Upon the mountaintop.

And then
The sun shone down,
Peekin' through the trees
Like God's great love

Shinin' just for me.

THE WORD

Then one of the elders asked me,

> "These in white robes—who are they,
> and where did they come from?"

I answered,

> "Sir, you know."

And he said,

> "These are they who have come out of the great tribulation;
> they have washed their robes and made them white
> in the blood of the Lamb.

Therefore,

> "they are before the throne of God
> > and serve him day and night in his temple;
> and he who sits on the throne
> > will shelter them with his presence.

> 'Never again will they hunger;

never again will they thirst.
The sun will not beat down on them,'
nor any scorching heat.

For the Lamb at the center of the throne
will be their shepherd;
'he will lead them to springs of living water.'
'And God will wipe away every tear from their eyes.'"

—Revelation 7:13-17

JARED

"The Hum of Silence"

I've heard the hum of silence
And come to fear its drone.
Sometimes it lasts mere seconds,
The time between seeing the IED and hearing the
BOOM.

Sometimes it lasts long hours,
The time between your APC exploding and when
rescue arrives.
The time between seeing the mountain
And climbing up its side.

I've heard the hum of silence
And come to fear its drone.
For in its fearsome echo,
I know I am alone.

ARIEL

They dressed us in white

And called us Little Angels

So happy, they wept

DINAH

"Angel in the Desert"

My robes were white

And people were nice

When I was an angel in the desert.

I found friends, many friends

Singing songs without ends

When I was an angel in the desert.

How we played

While Mommy prayed

When I was an angel in the desert

The spirit contagious

Our laughter outrageous

When I was an angel in the desert.

We watched the skies

With sleepy-kid eyes

When I was an angel in the desert.

How I cried, how I cried,

Faced with truths and with lies

When I was an angel in the desert.

I lost friends, many friends

Who I'll never see again

When I was an angel in the desert.

I questioned the meaning of faith,

But I always felt safe

When I was an angel in the desert.

I'll never forget,

And I'll never regret

When I was an angel in the desert.

TOBY

MASADA

A Loving Community of Faith

Are you ready for Christ's return?

Join us!

Visitors halt at checkpoint

TRESPASSERS WILL BE SHOT

ARIEL

Our utopia

Waited for God's great kingdom

With endless labor

MARY

"Notes of Hope"

The congregation came to shout
The Lord his due under the sun.
Sunburned, tired, they all came out
To music played on my organ.

Masada had become our home,
That lonely mountaintop our church.
Its ceiling was a bright blue dome,
Where Jesus smiled up on his perch.

For three long years they wait'd to live
As princes with God's princely son.
Hungry, spent, nothing left to give
They worshipped with great emotion.

And as they'd stagger back down the slope,
I'd still play them notes of hope.

RUTH

"Away From Town, An' Closer to the Lord"

I once believe'd I'd die alone
Away from my sons
Stuck in a place
So far from home.

But I am loved again
I am Grandma now
To the forgotten
To the lost an' broken.

I watch'd our lovin' flock grow
Swollen under the sun
Most had no faith
I cry'd watchin' them go.

Father show'd us to the wild

Amongst the beasts

We lived as Jesus had

Evr'y man, woman, child.

Away from town an' closer to the Lord

Father preach'd endlessly

Of sins an' serpents

An' dyin' by the sword.

He saw our sins so deep inside

He promis'd to cleanse us all

In the eyes of God

Of our jealousies an' pride.

JOSHUA

"Behind Our Walls, the Stones Are Bleeding"

I used to knock on doors

Spreading the holy word,

But now

We turn strangers away.

And behind our walls we stay.

I had love in my heart

And faith in my soul,

But now

I cannot feel God's power.

Behind our walls we cower.

Father says

We're to cleanse ourselves

And like Jesus live,

But I think he wants more
Than I can give.

Those outside are full of sin,
Inside we're full of fear,
And now
We all know someone lied.
Behind our walls we hide.

My enthusiasm is drained
My curiosity beaten,
And now
I want to run away.
But behind our walls I stay.

Father says
We're to cleanse ourselves
And like Jesus live,
But I think he wants more
Than anyone can give.

JEDIDIAH

Things didn't go bad,

Things went good.

You say we fell mad out there,

But I say we found sanity.

Where you see horror,

I remember beauty.

You say:

The congregation toiled,

And they hungered,

And they thirsted,

And they suffered,

Like it's a bad thing.

Yes, they toiled and suffered,

Yes, they hungered and thirsted,

Because they loved God.

To be good enough for the Lord.

To be like Christ himself.

Name one thing nobler than that.

Jesus hadn't come,

And David knew why.

We weren't entitled to the kingdom,

No, we had to earn it.

He knew what had to be done:

To be like Christ, each man had to be without sin.

Hate the sin, love the sinner—

That was my motto.

The Fishers set out to accomplish the great task

Of making each man like Christ worthy of Christ's

kingdom.

And everything David and I and the Fishers did

We did out of the purest love.

THE WORD

Those whom I love

I rebuke and discipline.

So be earnest and repent.

—Revelation 11:15

ARIEL

God would wipe our tears

But first we had to make them

I tried to be good

GABRIEL

"The Watchers"

The Reverend told us there were people out there
Who want to stop us rising up in the air
Who'd like nothing more to keep us chained to the
ground
To put us all back where we were found

Now I'd come too far to think of going back
Jed gave us rifles and he put us on track
He told my crew we're coming to the end
You're my Watchers now, and it's you I will send

To be a watcher, a shepherd, a spreader of news
A fighter, a marshal, a runner of crews
A savior, a king, a solver of clues
A sword, a shield, a counter of coups

We put up barbed wire and we held the line

All of us Watchers numbered nine

Few allowed in, nobody leaving

Those who sinned were soon grieving

Matthew tried to go and we broke his bones

We left another fool to rot on the stones

The Rev said God willed we defend

Our hopes and future, it was on me he'd depend

To be a watcher, a shepherd, a spreader of news

A fighter, a marshal, a runner of crews

A savior, a king, a solver of clues

A sword, a shield, a counter of coups

MARY

"Eye of the Needle"

My sin was pride, I know that now.
The Reverend Prince, he saw that clear.
My pretty music refused to bow.
I'm no good to see, but great to hear.

I stroked the keys to talk to God,
To help my brethren wait with cheer.
But God wouldn't come if we were flawed,
If we held on what we each held dear.

The Reverend, he said he must
Cut off my fingers there and here.
I watched the man I gave my trust
Them chop while Jesus felt so near.

Then David kissed me while I cried
My thanks he'd rescued me from pride.

THE WORD

And if your eye causes you to sin,

Gouge it out and throw it away.

It's better to enter eternal life

With only one eye

Than to have two eyes

And be thrown

Into the fire of hell.

—Mathew 18:9

DINAH

"Me, Mommy, and Masada"

In the trees, in the trees

Something is happening,

But no one can see.

We have walls, such tall walls

We never have visitors,

But at night I hear coyote calls.

My robes so bright and white

Air so fresh and clean,

But Mommy cries at night.

I miss Mary playing the organ

Some people are sad,

But I mostly feel boredom.

Sometimes only us Angels eat

Some people are hungry,

Try to leave and get beat.

I asked Mommy if we could leave

She told me no,

That soon we'd be free.

In the trees, in the trees

Something is happening,

But no one can see.

JARED

"We All Have Our Jobs to Do"

We all have our jobs to do
To support this family,
See our calling through.

Mary played the organ
With great grace and skill.
Luke grew a garden
To keep our bellies filled.

Aaron, Daniel, and Martha
Cut down lots of trees.
Clearing plots of land,
Building homes for families.

Washing ladies did laundry

Washed the Angels' robes of white.

Father and the Fishers

Praying through the night.

Ruth cared for the children

With patience and with love.

Watchers were our wardens

Watching from above.

Joshua's spirit darkened

While I worked on the wall.

They chopped Mary's fingers off

No one said anything at all.

We all have our jobs to do

To support this family,

See our calling through.

TOBY

Toby, come here!
Toby, carry this!
Toby, it's time to sleep!
Toby, they need help in the fields!
Toby, it's time for prayers!
Toby, turn out your lantern and go to sleep!
Toby, wake up!
Toby, get some water from the river!
Toby, you sing like an angel!
Toby, come here and help us hold him down!
Toby, hold him good!
Toby, turn away and don't look!
Toby, stop crying.

ARIEL

Matthew tried to run

They broke his knees with a crack!

To keep his soul put

ELIZABETH

"A Cure for What Ails You"

We didn't wait, we fought a war
Against sin both inside and out.
The Reverend had just the cure.

I was ugly inside, of that I was sure,
But outside my beauty did flout,
The flesh corrupt, my soul made pure.

The lusts of men my beauty did lure,
Looks and lusts God could do without.
The Reverend had just the cure.

The Reverend had me held to the floor,
Knife in hand, Jed knifed my pout,
The flesh corrupt, my soul made pure.

Jed sliced my face and said now you're
The same girl both inside and out.
The Reverend had just the cure.

It hurt, it hurt, I wanted more,
Cut it away, I tried to shout,
The flesh corrupt, my soul made pure.
The Reverend had just the cure.

APOCALYPSE

August 17, 2008

JEDIDIAH

August 17. The long last night.

That's what you want to hear about, right?

That's all that matters to you.

The suicides, the murders.

Crazies doing what crazies do.

That's what you want to hear.

And the fact you do

Is why we did it.

We didn't want to do it.

We didn't want to die after all that hard work.

What we wanted,

What we'd worked so hard for years to achieve,

What we'd all sacrificed parts of ourselves for—

Our minds and flesh,

Our eyes and tongues and fingers—

Was entrance into Christ's earthly kingdom.

What David realized,

When the congregation could give no more,

After nine had already died,

Was we were already ready.

We weren't waiting for Jesus.

Jesus was waiting for us.

All we had to do was shed our mortal coil,

Allow our purified spirits to ascend to God.

I heard David praying, begging,

Pleading with God to take this burden from him.

But while Jesus forgives everything,

His father demands everything.

God wanted the ultimate sacrifice.

A sacrifice of blood.

And if we, like Christ, gave it with an open heart,

The kingdom would open to us

While the world burned to make room for

something new.

THE WORD

I saw thrones on which were seated
Those who had been given authority to judge.

And I saw the souls of those who had been
beheaded
Because of their testimony about Jesus and
Because of the word of God.

They had not worshiped the beast or its image
And had not received its mark on their foreheads or
their hands.

They came to life and reigned with Christ a thousand years.

—Revelation 20:4

JEDIDIAH

"Charge the Gates of Heaven"

David Prince came to me,
Whispering in the dark.
Telling me of truths he'd learned
A great destiny we'd hark.

He told me then,
In breathless voice,
We'd charge the gates of heaven great
We'd make the final choice.

He spoke to God above,
Basking in his light.
And God showed him then
What had been blind to his sight.

He told me then,
In his gentle way,
To charge the gates of heaven great
We all must perish today.

RUTH

"God and Gold"

After my sons sold my home,
And tuck'd me away to die,
I had some gold for rainy days
But I was alone by and by.

When our shepherd call'd me
To shed my gold and pride
I gladly gave it all to him
To stand right by his side.

When we reach'd our new home
So high up in the trees
I need'd neither gold nor sons
Just God's refreshing breeze.

After we learn'd our destiny
A choice so hard and bold
I felt my heart swell up with joy
I learned about God and gold.

MARY

"Come, Lord Jesus"

My David, he called us around,
He said that now the time had come,
Cast mortal flesh onto the ground,
Let spirit fly up to the sun.

The day of victory was at hand,
The kingdom, it was coming fast,
And once our blood soaked into sand,
Our spiritual war was won at last.

I longed to make my suffer'ng end,
To rise to God and take my seat,
Instead I hid to avoid my friends,
Because it felt like one big cheat.

I still had pride, I do agree,
But Jesus should have come to me.

JOSHUA

"Failed Prophet"

I am afraid my faith
Has turned on me
And eaten up my hope.
We are hiding now
But from what
I do not know.

I am afraid of the others,
My brothers and sisters,
And how they'll cope.
We are isolated now,
From the world,
And all we've known.

I am afraid my prophet
Has failed me
And led me far astray.
He tells us now
We must die
To end the world today.

ARIEL

Something wonderful
Is coming, Mommy said, and
Hid me in a crate

ELIZABETH

"Judgment Day"

Cut off your hand if it goes astray,
The Reverend said in the heat.
Today, he said, is Judgment Day.

So take and drink, this is the way,
To burn the chaff and save the wheat.
Expose the soul, our flesh must flay.

I took my cup, ready to pay,
Ready to rise and take my seat.
Today, he said, is Judgment Day.

Pretended drink but chose delay,
Immediate salvation I did cheat.
Expose the soul, our flesh must flay.
I feigned death while some ran away,

With guns the Watchers did them greet.

Today, he said, is Judgment Day.

I tell you truly, I must say,

I'm not worthy yet for Christ to meet.

Expose the soul, our flesh must flay.

Today, he said, is Judgment Day.

RUTH

"Come to Grandma Now" (Reprise)

Look at all the little children

Our angels of innocence

Surviv'd cruel world

In this age of Leviticus.

Come to Grandma now

Let me love you like my own.

We've all been through much

Pain has bond'd us

We are family now

Held tight with love an' trust.

Come to Grandma now

Let our love take us home.

138

Look at all the little children

So brave now at the End

The drinks are sitting all mix'd up

We're ready to transcend.

Come to Grandma now

Children we'll never be alone.

We've all learn'd the truth

Now there's no need for tears

We're sacrificin' ourselves

To save them all, my dears.

Come to Grandma now

Let God's work be done.

Look at all the good children

Drinkin' from their cups

Such still reverent babies

I love you all so much.

Come to Grandma now

Let me love you like my own.

MARY

"No Goodbyes"

From where I hid I saw it clear,
The hundreds all lined up to die.
They drank the dark punch without fear,
There was no need to say goodbye.

I saw them all fall to the dirt,
Dying bodies shook like Shakers.
Later Toby rose unhurt,
I saw he was among the fakers.

Regret, despair, myself forlorn,
My life betrayed my faith, the rest.
But yes, I could be quite stubborn,
The Lord already had my best.

When God asks me, I'll tell him true,
I'd already come to you.

TOBY

I'm not

As

Dumb

As everybody

Thought

I was.

DINAH

"Mommy's Sharp Kiss Goodbye"

Father Prince told us we were special

In the eyes of God.

And everyone believed him,

Especially my mom.

Mommy held me tight as they

Handed out the punch.

But when it came to us

I resisted it at once.

Father Prince told us we must sacrifice

In the name of God.

And everyone believed him,

Especially my mom.

Mommy drew a knife

When I spilt my punch.

She held it to my throat

As she told me to hush.

Father Prince told us we were Heaven bound

To his loving God.

And everyone believed him,

Especially my mom.

I fought for my life

While the rest went Heaven bound.

Mommy raised the knife,

And then she brought it down.

Father Prince told us we were special,

That we were saving the world.

And everyone believed him,

Except this little girl.

Mommy bled out

While the others gagged on punch.

I hid under her body,

And she finally saved me for once.

ARIEL

Singing to Dolly,

"Mommy's coming back soon, dear"

After the first screams

GABRIEL

"Last Night on Earth"

They drank the elixir, put the bags on their heads

One by one, they all dropped dead

Women and men, girls and boys

They had to die first to discover the joys

Of the great kingdom where the angels tread

Through Heaven's gate where the right path led

Heaven awaits, the Reverend said

To pass through the eye one has to be thread

Some, they said, they didn't want to show

The Rev, he just couldn't let them go

He loved them too much to fail them now

He's given orders and that was how

We watched them run as fast as they can

Adam and Isaac, Chloe and Anne,

We took up rifles and shot them as they ran

We're all going together—that was the plan

Some, they didn't die right away

Jed said we had to send them off on their way

He took up an axe and started the chopping

Even for the kids there was no stopping

The screaming, the crying, the pleading for grace

Jed started chopping at a steady pace

Then cut off their heads just in case

He delivered them from their mortal disgrace

After that, we went to search for more

Then the Rev, he said it's time he go through the door

He'd been there watching all the while

Now it was time to depart in style

We crucified him as day turned to night

Do it now, he said, you do it right

We doused him with gas, a match did ignite

The Reverend screamed as he went alight

The last screams died as the fire waned

The Rev up in Heaven beginnin' his reign

The Watchers each shot themselves in the brain

I survived the bullet and so I remain

A watcher, a shepherd, a spreader of news

A fighter, a marshal, a runner of crews

A savior, a king, a solver of clues

A sword, a shield, a counter of coups

JARED

"My Cup Untouched"

I watched them mixing the cups
With a sick feeling in my gut.
Sacrifice reeked of toxins
As life is rotted with sin.
Sweet old Ruth gave me mine,
Pink plastic cup with poison inside.

I held my Bible, hands trembling,
Looking around at our reckoning.
People convulsing and dying,
Prince's orders, all complying.
Guns at the gates, bags over heads,
Making sure that they're all dead.

In the chaos, I saw Joshua run
Seconds later, I heard Gabriel's gun.
I tried to be brave and just take a drink
"But I'm still alive" was all I could think.
I couldn't drink, and I couldn't flee,
Witnessing Father burn, Watchers and me.

I stared at death, willing but unable,
I saw my past so steady and stable.

"But I'm still alive" was all I could think
I stood up, limped away from my drink.
Past Joshua bleeding in the dirt.
Past Gabriel, gun down and eyes hurt.

I limped through a field of the dead,
Limped to the gate, cold with dread.
I turned back once, for one final look
At the chair where I'd sat, my cup and my book.
The Bible open, the cup undisturbed,
Prince wrong again, this wasn't deserved.

JEDIDIAH

"SAVING 343 Souls in a Single Day"

I.

Father Prince led us in prayer.

And as our last AMEN echoed,

Peter slit his wrists

All the way to the bone.

II.

I heard the instructions

Father gave the Watchers:

KILL those who do not die

He said, over and over.

III.

Six Fishers remained

But only four prepared the punch

Because Seth and Mark

Went to drown themselves

In the BAPTIZING creek.

IV.

I heard gunfire and screams,

And I could hear everyone

Gagging, vomiting, DYING

As I watched the sun fall.

V.

At sundown

Father Prince was CRUCIFIED

On a cross of weathered pine.

On his orders

The Watchers doused him

With Gasoline.

He burned,

How he burned,

Oh, holy pyre

Oh, cleansing fire.

Taking away

Our martyred Father.

VI.

I walked amongst them

Ending their MISERIES,

And sending them to a Heaven

With the ax from the shed.

The Lord, he told me,

To take their heads.

VII.

I sent six souls to HEAVEN myself

Before I drank my cup,

The Devil reached down my throat

And made me throw it up.

VIII.

I woke up shackled,

Shameless in my sacrifice,

Yet swallowed by sadness.

I am unrepentant,

So they call my devotion

MADNESS.

ARIEL

Everybody dead
But I never found my Mommy
She lives with God now

THE WORD

Then I saw "a new heaven and a new earth,"
For the first heaven and the first earth had passed away,
And there was no longer any sea.

I saw the Holy City,
The New Jerusalem,
Coming down out of Heaven from God,
Prepared as a bride beautifully dressed for her husband.

And I heard a loud voice from the throne saying,

"Look! God's dwelling place is now among the people,
And he will dwell with them.
They will be his people,
And God himself will be with them and be their God.

"'He will wipe every tear from their eyes.
There will be no more death'

Or mourning or crying or pain,

For the old order of things has passed away."

—Revelation 21:1-4

JOSHUA

"Seasons"

This Summer is fire,
Autumn shall be ash,
And Winter a long restless sleep
In a room with no ceiling.

Maybe Spring will wake us,
Or maybe let us toss and turn,
But either way I have to say,
I trust the Seasons no more.

ARIEL

It was all nothing

I mean it was all for naught

It was everything

JEDIDIAH

I wonder how Noah felt,
Building an ark in the middle of land.
Shouting a warning nobody heard,
Leaving the world behind to drown.

I wonder how Moses felt,
Looking at the Promised Land.
Knowing he could not enter,
Watching his stubborn children go.

I wonder how Judas felt,
Betraying his master to save the world.
Looking at his crucified king,
Accepting he was cursed to Hell.

I wonder how Abraham felt,
Asked by God to kill his son.
After his release he looked at his knife
And knew exactly who he was.

ELIZABETH

"The Final Victory"

They killed them with poison and with the gun,

By slaying their flesh, their souls are now free.

With sacrifice will God's victory be won.

David was wrong, his win comes for none,

Sacrifice and death for more is key.

We obey the Lord, and his will be done.

Behold, our beloved world's end will come,

When every sinner has come to agree,

With sacrifice will God's victory be won.

My mission is continue what was begun,

I will show them if they just follow me.

We obey the Lord, and his will be done.

What happened at Masada a nation did stun,

But our faith and love allowed many to see,

With sacrifice will God's victory be won.

So now I've become a church of one,

I'll renew the work and save the many.

We obey the Lord, and his will be done.

With sacrifice will God's victory be won.

MARY

"Come, Lord Jesus"

We didn't fly up to the sky,
Our great mission horribly failed.
But I am glad we made the try,
And everything that it entailed.

The hunger, torture, and final death,
I face my past without regret.
I'll love the Family to my last breath,
And drown despair in Percocet.

Sometimes, I lay in bed at night,
And I will dream a bright blue day.
The sinners raise hands to the light,
While smiling, I my organ play.

The Family lived and died in strife,
Truly, the best time of my life.

JARED

"After the Funerals"

After the massacre came the cameras

After the cameras came the funerals

After the funerals came the silence

And now, here I dwell,

In my personal hell,

Alone in the great silence.

RUTH

"Ghosts"

Again, I'm alone.
Surround'd by ghosts,
Sufferin' remorse,
In my new home.

Again, I'm alone.
Flowers on the wall,
Faded yellow tulips,
In my new home.

Again, I'm alone.
Meals are on time,
Pills at 3, 6, and 9,
In my new home.

Again, I'm alone,

Guards in the hall,

Clubs on their hips,

In my new home.

Again, I'm alone.

I've abandon'd my fear,

Knowin' I'll die here,

In my new home.

JOSHUA

"How Long Have We Been Bleeding From Our Hands?"

I knew it was going bad

When we turned people away.

I could feel it in the air,

Taste it in the water.

I tried to leave the camp,

Nowhere to go, but couldn't stay.

They brought me back,

And beat me

In front of everyone.

How can this be happening?

How can we be falling apart at our seams?

I knew my bruises would heal

But that I could never be free.

Our light has grown dim,

Our love gotten sharper.

I wanted to leave the camp,

When Ruth passed the cup to me.

I broke for the gate,

And felt bullets

Shatter

My

Spine—

How could this be happening?

How could we be falling apart at our seams?

How could I be so blind?

They say I'll never walk again

And I know I'll never pray.

I watched all the faithful,

I watched them all die.

Now looking back at camp

I can cry, but know not what to say.

Now I'm all alone

And broken

With only questions.

How long has this been happening?

How long have we been falling apart at out seams?

How long have I been so blind?

How long have we been bleeding from our hands?

JEDIDIAH

I killed Thomas with an axe

Then I killed Luke, then more

I cut off their heads

And I loved them, so

I lost something too

You say: But what did you really lose, Jed?

Mary lost her fingers, Elizabeth her beauty

John his eyes; everybody made an offering

What did you give?

The simple truth is everything

I can't enter the kingdom with blood on my hands

I killed my friends so they could go

I gave up my chance so they'd have theirs

I loved them enough

That I couldn't see them left behind

175

Sometimes I look

Out through my jail bars

And I see the morning sun

And think it's fire, and I

See the apocalypse coming

When the last of us are dead

God's wrath will burn the world

And all the Family of God will enter the kingdom

One day I'll have the courage to

Make my last sacrifice for them

Come, Lord Jesus

Amen

DINAH

"Nothing, No One"

I'm an orphan again,
My robes
No longer soft and
White,
But stiff and faded
Blue.
Maybe that's because
I want
Nothing
From no one.
And I speak
Only in
Poetry.
And talk
Only to
You.

THE AUTHORS

Craig DiLouie is the author of nine novels, notably *Suffer the Children, The Retreat, The Infection, The Killing Floor,* and *Tooth and Nail.* He has also contributed short fiction to a number of anthologies. Learn more about Craig's fiction at CraigDiLouie.com.

Jonathan Moon is the author of 16 novels, novellas and short story collections, notably *Worms in the Needle, Heinous, Hollow Mountain Dead, Cannibal Hunter,* and *Stories to Poke Your Eyes Out to.* He has also contributed short fiction to a number of anthologies. Learn more about Jonathan's fiction at MrMoonBlogs.blogspot.com

55176708R00112

Made in the USA
Charleston, SC
20 April 2016